The Simple Guide to Sensitive Boys

also in the Simple Guides series

The Simple Guide to Child Trauma
What It Is and How to Help
Betsy de Thierry
Illustrated by Emma Reeves
Foreword by David Shemmings
ISBN 978 1 78592 136 0
eISBN 978 1 78450 401 4

of related interest

Promoting Young Children's Emotional Health and Wellbeing
A Practical Guide for Professionals and Parents
Sonia Mainstone-Cotton
ISBN 978 1 78592 054 7
eISBN 978 1 78450 311 6

How to Parent Your Anxious Toddler
Natasha Daniels
ISBN 978 1 84905 738 7
eISBN 978 1 78450 148 8

The Gender Agenda
A First-Hand Account of How Girls and Boys Are Treated Differently
Ros Ball and James Millar
Foreword by Marianne Grabrucker
ISBN 978 1 78592 320 3
eISBN 978 1 78450 633 9

Be Bully Free
A Hands-On Guide to How You Can Take Control
Michael Panckridge and Catherine Thornton
ISBN 978 1 78592 282 4
eISBN 978 1 78450 583 7

Banish Your Self-Esteem Thief
A Cognitive Behavioural Therapy Workbook on Building Positive Self-Esteem for Young People
Kate Collins-Donnelly
ISBN 978 1 84905 462 1
eISBN 978 0 85700 841 1

Outsmarting Worry
An Older Kid's Guide to Managing Anxiety
Dawn Huebner PhD
Illustrated by Kara McHale
ISBN 978 1 78592 782 9
eISBN 978 1 78450 702 2

The Simple Guide to Sensitive Boys

How to Nurture Children and Avoid Trauma

BETSY DE THIERRY

Foreword by Jane Evans

Illustrated by Emma Reeves

Jessica Kingsley *Publishers*
London and Philadelphia

First published in 2018
by Jessica Kingsley Publishers
73 Collier Street
London N1 9BE, UK
and
400 Market Street, Suite 400
Philadelphia, PA 19106, USA

www.jkp.com

Front cover image source: Emma Reeves

Library of Congress Cataloging in Publication Data
A CIP catalog record for this book is available from the Library of Congress

British Library Cataloguing in Publication Data
A CIP catalogue record for this book is available from the British Library

ISBN 978 1 78592 325 8
eISBN 978 1 78450 639 1

Printed and bound in Great Britain

To Jeremy, Andrew, Josh, Ben, Jonah and Noah.

CONTENTS

FOREWORD

This observation in Betsy de Thierry's innovative and thought-provoking exploration of boys and their sensitivity and emotional needs is the one we should all have pinned up somewhere:

> 'Boys do cry. Girls also cry. Some children cry more than others.'

As a society we currently do our boys a real disservice by teaching them to 'man-up' and 'stop crying like a girl'. This book serves as a much-needed reminder of why so many of our boys are sensitive and why this should be widely embraced. Instead, all too often, these boys are stressed from trying to cope, in a range of unhealthy ways, with their suppressed feelings. This fails them; it also has wider implications for society.

Betsy makes the much-needed point that boys and girls feel what they feel. Some are more sensitive than others, but this is not attributable purely to their gender! Male suicide is the biggest killer of our boys and men under 45 years of age.

Of the total number of suicides (6,188 deaths) registered in the UK in 2015, three quarters (75%) were males and one quarter (25%) were females (Office for National Statistics 2015). Raising boys to hide or deny their feelings must surely feed into this?

It is time for a serious rethink throughout our society, and Betsy is leading the way with her clear messages and insight both as a parent of four boys but also from her work with boys who display trauma through their behaviour whilst seemingly not having experienced what we recognise as trauma.

Through her reflective questions, Betsy invites us to be actively involved in addressing the needs of boys who are sensitive. She creates ways to be curious and to challenge how and why boys are trapped into showing up in life in a certain predefined 'masculine' way. It is abundantly clear this is failing so many of our boys and men, leaving them to push down their feelings and present in ways that lead to high levels of stress and, for far too many, mental and physical illness. Others stagger on for too long, self-medicating in 'socially acceptable' ways that are addictive, numbing and create a multiplicity of problems at home, work, in the community and in society (e.g. alcohol, food, social media).

I am grateful to Betsy for addressing boys' sensitivity head on. When I worked with teenage boys who were being abusive to their parents, I repeatedly discovered that they were highly sensitive and had high levels of toxic stress from their early childhood experiences. My hope is that a copy of this book will be everywhere that boys and those raising them can be found, and that it becomes THE gift to a family every time a boy is born.

Jane Evans

Speaker, trainer and author specialising in the support of children's mental health

Chapter 1

UNDERSTANDING SENSITIVE BOYS

In some ways it is hard to define a 'sensitive boy' because we are all sensitive.

However, boys can have a particularly hard time if they are sensitive. They can be misunderstood, bullied, isolated and feel disconnected from friends, their dreams and the ability to live a life being who they authentically feel that they are.

The idea for this simple guide arose from the work that I do with children who are struggling in some way. I'm a psychotherapist and teacher and run several charities dedicated to working with troubled families.

Some of the children I see have experienced significant trauma in their early lives, but, increasingly, I have noticed that others have no known trauma history and yet still exhibit signs of stress – in some cases toxic stress, which is a severity of stress usually found in children who have experienced early abuse, and which can affect brain architecture and chemistry. Trauma is defined by Perry (2011) as 'a psychologically distressing event that is outside the range of usual human experience, often involving a sense of intense fear, terror and helplessness' (cited in de Thierry 2015, p.21).

As I encountered this more frequently in families where parents were worried about their sons, I started to ask questions.

> Does this boy react strongly, really enjoy or engage with music, stories or art?
>
> Does this boy seem to have very deep emotional responses to things?
>
> Does this boy show deep empathy for others' emotions and situations?
>
> Does this boy prefer reading, writing, singing, drawing or talking to playing football?
>
> Does this boy seem to ask deeper questions about life than many of his peers?

These are hardly complex clinical questions, but they enabled me to get a sense of how some of these boys are wired and how they may struggle with a culture that seems to make an assumption that all boys will equally love football and enjoy physical play with each other.

> The creative mind is wired with the ability to feel with great depth and passion. Without good strategies for managing this hypersensitivity, instead of creativity the result can be a plunge into the emotional depths. (Crabtree and Crabtree 2011, p.69)

Every child can be easily hurt by damaging relationships, rejection, hurtful words, nasty experiences, betrayal, insecurity, uncertainty or other such frightening experiences. However, each child will respond differently and the depth of impact will depend on several factors, including the child's primary relationships and personality. Some are much more sensitive than others and will have less resilience (i.e., ability to recover from difficult experiences), due to their character, which may be inherited or influenced by experience. For example, a child who struggles to join in group activities can also struggle to build a sense of self-confidence and this can be for a number of reasons.

We have all encountered the well-trodden debate relating to how children become who they are – nature (inherited qualities) or nurture (environmental influences). Most agree that both play a part, but there is also broad agreement that some children are born with a 'thicker skin' and have greater natural resilience than others.

Our expectation of men and boys

As a mother of four boys, each so completely different and some more sensitive than others, I have been staggered at the expectations placed on each one. I've witnessed in different schools, in a span of 20 years of parenting, how sporty, fast, aggressive boys are celebrated and musical, gentle, creative, sensitive boys are seen as the exception and almost to be worried about. I have seen that boys have to find extraordinary resilience to be bold enough to be confident in their brilliant uniqueness. I have witnessed teachers, parents and others who have influence in a child's life continually reinforcing the need for boys to be tough, emotionless and care mostly about sport. They do it subtly by the raising of eyebrows, the sighs, the comparisons, the sports day eagerness, the conversations, and it can result in confused looks on the faces of parents who are missing out on the genius of their children because they so want to 'fit in' to the norms of our society.

Thankfully, Brené Brown, a research professor at the University of Houston Graduate College of Social Work, is raising awareness about the small boxes we put boys into from an early ages:

> We keep them trapped by rewarding, reinforcing and punishing. We reward their willingness to stay in the box by celebrating their 'toughness' and reinforce and punish by labelling any demonstration of vulnerability or emotion (especially fear, grief, and sadness) as weakness. (Brown 2008, p.281)

All boys are sensitive and thus the information in this book is relevant to every boy, but some are more sensitive than others and struggle more than others. My hope is that the advice in this book will help to make a difference between a sensitive boy living a life of turmoil or a life of adventure.

As a society we love to cherish and adore babies. When they are that small, fragile and vulnerable, it's hard to imagine the kind of ceilings and boxes that will almost definitely become a reality when they lose their baby soft cheeks. As soon as they can begin to speak and own their opinion, the world seems to take pleasure in informing each individual child how they should be, what they should feel and how they should present themselves to the world going forward. This is achieved through the constant media input, through conversations directed at the child or around the child, through the constant barrage of images on toy packages and through TV that reinforces the implicit message of society's expectations for each child. With little boys, once they are old enough to shout, we seem to delight in subtly helping them to hide all vulnerability, weakness, gentleness or sensitivities and instead respond with understanding and humour when they display aggressive, tough behaviours.

> Based on participants' stories, it seems that father and male peers can be especially wounding to boys and men who stray from the norms of masculinity. (Brown 2008, p.282)

We need to take time to reflect on our definition of 'masculine' and our implicit, subconscious expectations of the boys and men around us, so that we can empower and support them to be the best that they can be. When we identify the children who are more sensitive, we are better able to support them and help them navigate through life with less emotional pain or turmoil, and we can offer them greater understanding and care.

We need the men that those sensitive boys will eventually become to take their place in our communities – they don't need fixing, but celebrating!

I like to picture what many of our nation-changers, celebrated musicians, artists, chefs, thinkers and writers were like as children. What were these adults, who we now recognise as creative geniuses, like at school? Did they have those tunes, films or books whirling about in their heads when they were meant to be listening in a maths lesson?

What about those intuitive and deep thinkers who have helped shape our thinking? Were they seen as slightly different? Did they confuse the other children, challenge the teachers or stimulate discussion that would never have had happened unless they were present?

Were the artists or musicians obviously creative when they were little? Were they highly sensitive to sound – perhaps they moaned about the assembly singing being out of tune? What about the thoughtful child who always had questions about the big issues of life whilst others were bickering about who could run the fastest? 'Sensitive boys are calmer, more thoughtful, and prefer to watch, test and experiment before they commit; but they are capable of fun and spontaneity' (Hartley-Brewer 2001, p.88).

Many sensitive children find school difficult because of a lack of common ground not only with peers, but also sometimes with teachers. Like parents, teachers need to understand how these children are different and celebrate their contribution to the class.

There is often a danger when we follow rules, when caring for children, which fail to recognise their individuality – this applies to our parenting and to teaching. When we expect them all to achieve similar results across a broad range of skills we can create an environment of pressure to 'be normal' and not leave any room for children to struggle in some areas and excel in others. Sensitive children can feel a sense of failure and a fear of expectation more deeply that other children and that can affect them adversely when learning.

While all schools are bound to teaching core subjects, it's unlikely that sensitive children will be able to show as much dedication to every subject as they do to their writing, music, art, thinking or deep care for others. Do sensitive boys have enough time to draw, sing, make, write, think or feel?

Overwhelm and turmoil

We can all become overwhelmed by too much stimulation,[1] too many things to think about or by too much happening.

We make sense of life is by processing stimuli; to do this we need to have time to process, think and

1 If your child reacts very strongly to sensory stimulation it is worth exploring sensory processing disorder (SPD), a condition in which the brain has trouble receiving and responding to information that comes in through the senses. Formerly referred to as sensory integration dysfunction (SID), it is not currently recognised as a distinct medical diagnosis by the DSM-5 but many children these days are identified as struggling with hypersensitivy to sensory stimulation, which can create real challenges as they interact with their worlds.

Please do research it further if children that you are in contact with are struggling with sound, touch, movement, sight, tastes or other experiences that other children don't seem to notice as challenging.

reflect on things that are happening to us. Some people prefer to do so verbally – by talking things through – others prefer to draw, write, sing, or spend time quietly thinking. Highly sensitive children can take longer to process stimuli if their natural method of processing isn't encouraged in the situation they are in.

If a child needs to sing to make sense of life and yet only quiet work is allowed in schools and singing is seen as distracting, then that child could become easily overwhelmed.

If a child dances to make sense of life and process strong feelings but they are told they have to sit still all day long with few opportunities for exercise, that child may start to behave in ways that are seen as defiant. They may run off to the toilets, fidget or jump around the classroom when they should be settled at their desk.

Although creative children are not the only ones who can be highly sensitive, there is research that evidences the way that they can become emotionally overwhelmed due to their hypersensitivity to emotion. When speaking about the specific sensitivities of creative people, psychologist and musician Crabtree and Crabtree write:

> they feel their own pain more intensely and feel others' pain as well. This is also based on the belief that creative people are not only better able to describe their own emotions, but they feel others' emotions more intensely. (Crabtree and Crabtree 2011, p.62)

I often use the image of buckets to explain feelings with the children I work with. I explain that we all – adults and children – carry around different buckets inside us.

Everyone has a shiny, golden bucket that collects love, happy moments, feelings of success and affirmations – encouraging, positive thoughts. The fuller the shiny bucket, the more stable and secure a child can feel.

Then there is the muddy bucket. This is where all the negative experiences collect and when life is too busy, the lid goes on and the contents of the bucket simmer until there is time to process them. Children demonstrate when they have full muddy buckets by their behaviour, and they need help to empty them. They will rarely ask for help articulately, through conversation; rather, they usually show the adults that they are struggling by their behaviour, unless an adult has spent time exploring and enabling them to use words that express emotional needs.

As adults, we know far too well what it is like to have a catastrophic event occur and then have to put those thoughts, feelings and worries in a bucket so that we can assume our professional roles during the day. At the end of the day there may be time to attend to the feelings or worries, and to be able to process the bucket's contents. But if we don't have time, and if more and more has gone into the bucket, then we can leak!

When we leak as adults we can become grumpy, irritable, tired or sad – and when we leak this can spill over and affect our colleagues, our family, or, if we work with children, it can affect them too.

Highly sensitive boys get 'full muddy buckets' quickly because of the depth of their feelings, unless they are familiar with ways of processing and emptying them early on and able to do this.

For example, if we know that Johnny needs to bash on his drums or keyboard when he gets home for an hour or two or else he will become angry, then we can incorporate that into the day. If we know that Michael needs to spend time writing in his journal, then that needs to be a priority!

Building resilience

Throughout this book we will be exploring what kind of things the adults around sensitive boys can do to help them develop strongly and with less confusion or emotional pain.

This book will often, but not exclusively, refer to boys whose sensitivity causes them to be unable to take part in team sports in a way that offers them the experience of a strong sense of belonging, acceptance and camaraderie. Those who are able to be part of team sports usually have the opportunity to grow in confidence and resilience and as such are less vulnerable, despite their sensitivities, compared to those who don't get to enjoy the strong sense of belonging to a male team. That is not to say that children who enjoy football and rugby can't be sensitive, but it can be difficult for a sensitive boy to navigate the tension of failure, risk, shame and other negative emotions that can be so closely associated with team sports for those who are less natural at them.

Being part of any kind of team, creative or sports, can cause a significant increase in resilience, which decreases the impact of sensitivity. It can often be more difficult for a sensitive boy to naturally feel included in a friendship group of boys, and especially a boys' sports team, and this in itself can lead to social isolation that in turn can cause deep and enduring toxic stress. For them to be a part of another team, a drama club, a music group, a band, or an art or DT group, for example, would really strengthen the sensitive boy's sense of belonging, community and self.

> By helping boys develop inner strength and by nurturing their sometimes fragile self esteem, we can help them to become happy, warm, generous, confident individuals, fathers, and contributors to our society in the future – to everyone's benefit, including their own. (Hartley-Brewer 2001, p.8)

In this book we will be exploring how to help a sensitive boy do really well at being them! We will look at how we can help them avoid overwhelm and enjoy life.

Chapter 2

HOW ARE BOYS DIFFERENT?

'Boys will be boys'

Having parented four sons who are completely different and having worked with many boys of all ages as a psychotherapist, I do find myself surprised that there are such strong expectations of what counts as normal behaviour for a boy.

It seems that there remains a strong belief that a 'true male' is someone who is sporty, interested in football and cares deeply about their strength and speed. I have found that boys in primary school classes still rate themselves against each other in terms of speed and sportiness. For young boys in many schools, the faster and stronger you are, the more popular and successful you are.

For those who don't lean towards a passion for sport there can be a sense of confusion early on. Little boys can feel immediately socially isolated if they can't join in with the conversation about the recent football game or if they don't show enthusiasm about it. Many pretend they have a passion and others do grow a love for sport. But there are also the boys who internalise all the confusion and anxiety that they feel regarding their identity, which is being taught to them by their peers at a tender age.

Similarly whilst many boys do seem to enjoy wrestling with each other physically, we need to remember that some do not. Some find it painful, invasive and intimidating and yet sometimes our culture seems to inform these boys that they are wrong and need to learn to wrestle and 'play roughly'.

'Boys don't cry'

Sadly, this is still a phrase you hear all too often and there is a common expectation that we need to toughen up our young boys by telling them not to cry. Perhaps this stems from an outdated belief that we need our men tough so they can fight in wars and work practically in our communities and therefore an overarching fear that maybe if we 'pander to their tears' they may become even 'weaker' or less 'useful' in these roles. Yet many boys will grow into adult men with careers that do not involve manual labour or military action; they will rely on their natural talent for being sensitive, creative, intuitive and deep for their adult paths. So why do so many communities seem to try to tease, shout down, laugh at and mock these talents rather than celebrate them and look forward to all the brilliance that these men will go on to create for future society.

Boys do cry. Girls also cry. Some children cry more than others. Some don't cry and instead they internalise their sadness, frustration and upset, which then go on to become areas of unexpressed turmoil and pain, lying dormant and poisonous in the souls of our sensitive boys.

Tears are a healthy way to express emotion and that does not change according to gender. However, they can be a huge inconvenience to others as social convention demands that we respond to rather than ignore them and thus they make it very difficult to avoid or deny the other person's emotional distress. Maybe that's part of the purpose. When we feel emotions that cause us to cry, we recover well when we connect with another person. We need community and we need others to validate our emotions and enable us to process them. Expressing feelings is not a feminine characteristic but the behaviour of a healthy person who is able to connect emotionally with others.

All children need to develop a sense of emotional courage where they can pick themselves up after a failure or rejection or disappointment. This resilience is becoming vital for children to learn in preparation for an adulthood that offers challenging and competitive work environments.

> Boys must learn how to be in touch with their own and other's feelings and perceptions because technological progress and greater global competition are creating jobs that require creative teamwork, collective problem solving, constant communication and joint approaches to risk. (Hartley-Brewer 2001, pp.7–8)

In the first Lego Movie there is a scene where Unikitty explains how much she loves Cloud Cuckoo Land, where she lives – the capital of rainbows and puppies. When asked about negative emotions she confidently tells the Lego characters that she pushes them 'down, down, down'. Not much further into the film, she becomes unsettled as she has these emotions that she is unfamiliar with bubbling up and then she explodes with anger. It's a funny scene that perfectly describes the dysfunction of pushing our emotions down for any length of time.

The important role of sensitive men in our society

Take a moment to ponder on the state of our communities if there were no male psychotherapists, mentors, youth workers, nurses, artists, film makers, musicians, writers, dancers, philosophers and all the other roles that are generally filled by sensitive, creative, intuitive, reflective males. How dull would the world be? Our communities thrive when we value and celebrate the individuals within them. Diversity should be enjoyed and should not be seen as a threat. Each child is unique, and we must recognise their uniqueness as something that will enhance the world they live in.

Yet, very often, little boys who show these gifts and skills can be teased, mocked, rejected, misunderstood and socially isolated. Gentleness should be celebrated as a sign of wisdom and sophistication and not labelled as non-male. How ridiculous…

Scientific evidence of male sensitivity

Recent research shows that:

- Boys mature more slowly than girls – they are slower to talk, to develop social skills and to develop physically.
- The pathways in the brain that regulate stress mature more slowly in boys, both before and after birth.
- Boys have fewer built-in mechanisms to deal with stress than girls. This means they are more affected by environmental stress – both before and after birth – than girls.

Therefore, this cultural tendency that can lead communities to be less emotionally engaging and nurturing to our baby boys needs to be arrested. We need to speak up and educate any adults who implicitly bully our young boys due to a subconscious fear that they will end up weak and not 'truly masculine'. Little boys need attuned, nurturing, gentle love and care from attachment figures who will celebrate them whomever they become and whatever their unique personality and specific talents.

So what is masculinity?

Society sends a strong message that masculinity is defined by physical strength and lack of emotional responses. It seems that most dictionaries avoid specifics and use phrases such as 'having qualities appropriate to or usually associated with a man' (Merriam-Webster 2017). Here is a definition from the Urban Dictionary:

> Often defined as aggressive, strong, and unfeeling or stoic. Being masculine means in modern times, at least, no shows of emotion, no flamboyance, no hugging or even looking at other men, must be interested in sports and physical/violent activity.
>
> What masculine is is simply what a man does. Assuming responsibility for your actions; being sympathetic, sensitive, and caring; and gentleness are perfectly fine for men. A true man is not a hard-nosed, violent, overgrown child; he's a mature, kind individual. (Urban Dictionary 2005)

Isn't this interesting to see the tension articulated in the Urban Dictionary between the expectations in our society of masculinity and the reality of what we value in men? If all our male psychotherapists, doctors, nurses, mentors and others in the caring professions felt uneasy with showing emotion and believed that physical activity or violence was a definition of masculinity, our society would be in a sorry state. If all the writers, poets, dancers, musicians and artists believed that they first had to wrestle with proving their manhood by being neutral in their emotions and aggressive, we would lose the vulnerability that enables such strong and powerful art, which enhances all our worlds, and which is created from their souls.

Every person has the natural ability to be gentle but also firm and tough. The polarity of our ways of being is what makes us such fascinating creatures. We must remind each other of our complexity and not limit our identities to small boxes that we have to try to squeeze into.

> When we fail to challenge young children's view of masculinity as associated only with power, aggression and control, the damage to individuals can be widespread. (Hartley-Brewer 2001, p.32)

People want to be powerful; powerlessness causes vulnerability. Boys need to explore their need for power and strength but the concept is more complex than is often presented by our media. Males often want to feel powerful, but it's good to remember power presents itself in different ways. Compare a noisy power tool that cuts down trees, where the sound echoes around in an invasive way, with the quiet but indisputable power of a river that cuts its path through rock.

What is truly masculine? Maybe every male has to work that out themselves, but, as adults, we need to make sure we don't offer a definition of masculinity that leads to confusion for, or pressure on, the sensitive boy.

Duncan's story

'Big boys don't cry' is a phrase I've come to hate. As a child, early primary school age, I would cry quite often. Maybe people got sick of me crying about things, or maybe they would handle issues differently. I don't know, but it forced me to suppress my feelings and not let them show. Also, I was never interested in playing sport. I preferred to draw, and find out about dinosaurs and animals. Sport, in this country, particularly football, is seen as such a definitive male activity that there's almost something wrong with you if you don't like it. I guess I enjoyed watching it. But not really playing it. I've always found the typical male stereotypes to be so different than me that I often feel like less of a man because of it. Very depressing and isolating. It really attacks one of your basic core biological identities. Not too long ago a friend openly thanked a nearby friend for being a 'manly man' that he could do manly things with. This felt really painful because I do not fit the role of sporty, burly, car-tinkering, bold, self-confident, mountaineering, hiking, just-walk-up-to-a-beautiful-woman-in-a-bar kind of guy.

I obsess over musical arrangements, and the vivid colours they produce in my head. The beautiful landscapes of sonic art that I can create.

Reflection points

1. How do I view masculinity?
2. Did I know that male babies are more sensitive before reading this? How will that change my understanding of the needs of boys?
3. What behaviour do I show when my muddy bucket is full? What helps me to 'empty the bucket'?

Chapter 3

FEELING DIFFERENT, FEELING REJECTED

'Sticks and stones may break my bones, but names will never hurt me?'

This was a familiar childhood rhyme that I was taught by my head teacher when I was crying about being teased at six years old. There is now research that reveals what takes place physiologically when a person experiences social rejection or social isolation and it shows that the popular rhyme is totally untrue (Hsu *et al.* 2013). Verbal abuse, teasing, social isolation, rejection and other negative social experiences cause the same response physiologically as physical harm.

Speaking life with our words

The words of a parent or other influential adult are powerful. The ancient wisdom of Proverbs 18.21 says: 'Death and life are in the power of the tongue.' Therefore, when a child hears his caregivers continually describe him as naughty or a troublemaker, his behaviour is likely to confirm their belief that this is true. I get quite cross about the labels and messages on boys' clothes which say 'troublemaker', 'bad boy', 'wild one' and other words that cause confusion to children about what behaviour is celebrated and expected for young males.

My staff and I have consistently found that when children hear us talk about them, both behind their back when they don't know that we know they are listening and when we talk to them directly, in a positive way, they seem to flourish as if they were thirsty plants who need water. So many children in therapy sessions speak of how they are 'bad', 'naughty' or 'irritating' and when we ask why they think that about themselves they tell us that they often hear the adults in their lives use those words about them. Some children ask us if we think they are bad inside and we tell all children that they are brilliant children who are trying to tell us something with their behaviour. We have had children introduce themselves to our team like this, 'Hello, I have anger management issues.' I always think that is devastating. Why would they live life with that label as their primary identity? We love to speak words of affirmation, and be specific in our encouragement to help them grow in confidence. We then love to watch as they develop and more clearly display the positive qualities we are saying they have.

The way we relate to a sensitive boy should be by using words of encouragement that empower him to be confident in his talents and individuality. The phrase 'sensitive boy' should not seen as a label that confines boys or puts a ceiling on them or limits positive expectations.

The impact of name-calling

As adults working with sensitive children, it is apparent that we must make sure that names are never used to shame children and we need to work hard with them to enable any words that are nasty not to 'stick' but to be shaken off. I strongly believe that for every one negative word spoken we need about twenty positive words to counteract the impact of the negative one, so the primary method of helping a child develop resilience around name-calling is to make sure that there are many adults speaking positive, affirming words about the child so that the few negative words fall away.

The need for emotional connection

We know that humans are born with a natural instinct to connect with other humans and there is increasing research that provides evidence of a baby's instinct to connect relationally. This contradicts the historic belief of health providers and parents that caring for the physical needs of the baby was sufficient for healthy growth. We know now that a baby needs relational connection all the way through their childhood and preferably with at least one consistent, nurturing, patient and loving adult (this is sometimes called a primary attachment relationship). Chapter 6 will look at the need for a child to experience this one significant adult who is able to provide an emotional security, which Bowlby (2006) described as a 'secure base' from which they can explore the world and develop into independent, healthy adults. Recent research, such as that of Perry (2006), shows that a child's brain development is influenced by the interactions they have in their early life. Healthy brain development, and the child's chances of growing into a happy, secure adult, are therefore dependent on positive, loving interactions with the people around them.

When a person senses rejection at any time through their babyhood and childhood, it impacts on their subconscious, their emotions and then subsequently their behaviour and relationships.

When a baby or a child feels rejection, whether it is explicit through words or actions or implicit through isolation, lack of interactions and lack of behaviour that demonstrates love and warmth, they absorb the negative feeling and it causes damage.

When a child who is more sensitive than others experiences rejection they can internalise turmoil, pain and hurt that can present many years later either as depression, anger or other strong negative feelings.

> Because we are social animals, other people are our primary sources of safety and stress. How others treat us has a direct and continuous impact on our sympathetic arousal. (Cozolino 2016, p.183)

Our sympathetic arousal is our physiological response to feelings of threat and fear, which will be explored in Chapter 5.

Rejection and physical pain

Many researchers have explored the idea that emotional reactions towards rejection share common physiological mechanisms with the physical experience of pain. MacDonald and Leary (2005) have termed the emotional reaction to rejection – where an individual perceives themself as either excluded, or devalued from a desired relational person/group – social pain. The resulting distress is commonly referred to as 'hurt feelings' (Leary and Springer 2001). The studies have shown which areas of the brain have been impacted by social isolation or perceived rejection and it is extraordinary to note that they are often the same areas that would be impacted if the person was hit or kicked or significantly injured.

When sensitive children experience rejection

When a sensitive child feels isolated from their peers due to feeling different or being misunderstood or just being unmotivated to follow the group, then they can feel deep emotional pain which can lead to one of two responses. One reaction is that they 'act out' their frustration and sadness by demonstrating it with aggression and anger in their behaviour. The other, which is a common response from sensitive children, is that they internalise their sadness which leads to either shutting down emotionally (becoming 'emotionally frozen') or dissociating or some other internal method of coping with such deep sadness. These will be explored in the next chapter as will ways to help a child respond in a healthier way.

The value of creativity

We live in a society that currently focuses heavily on academic performance and has strong expectations for every age in every subject. Again, I question how someone who is especially skilled in a specific subject is expected, and often pushed hard, to be 'national average' at everything.

Creativity brings life to communities. It breathes life to ugly, tired, dull places. Music, art, dance, film, graphics, stories and all other creative mediums light up our world and bring connection to hope and to each other. Sadly, these subjects are often referred to in our education system as 'softer subjects', which implies that they are easier than those that are perceived to be 'academic subjects', and indicates that pretty much everyone is capable of producing complex musical arrangements and creating art that brings life in places of pain such as hospitals. Why would our creative subjects be seen as easier or less appropriate for males to be committed to?

Being a creative boy brings challenges on so many levels in our current society. It can bring social isolation, misunderstanding, a feeling of confusion and sadness. Creativity brings with it a sensitivity that other children don't always share:

> Creative people are by definition those who see, sense, feel and perceive their inner and outer world more intently and more intensely. They take in more sensory information, which becomes the fuel for their creativity... This produces two opposing forces that act on the creative person: firstly, their sensitivity to pain and, in particular, their sensitivity to the pain of their world, and secondly, the pressure to take risks, to confront, to challenge and experience. (Crabtree and Crabtree 2011, p.69)

We refer to successful creative adults as celebrities and speak highly of their skills and are grateful for how they have contributed to our society with their films, music, art, performances, writing and philosophical thinking. Did we show them the same level of respect and encouragement when they were at school? Do you think they had the same kind of focus or interests in things that other boys at school pushed to have as a common interest? Did we support their sensitive natures? Did we recognise their sensory overwhelm and support them in the process of making sense of how they feel?

The sense of belonging

Children are emotionally healthy when they experience the feeling of long-term belonging, for example to a group or a team or a club. When they feel that sense of 'brotherhood' and peer affirmation when they are growing up, they will develop significantly more resilience and will be less likely to seek out negative group dynamics when they are adolescents. As adults, we need to be imaginative in trying to create groups for children to belong to (for example, a drama club, music group or story-writing group where like-minded children can meet regularly) where they don't feel on the edge or unusual or different, but rather they feel accepted and a strong sense of belonging.

Anne's story

I am Mum to a sensitive boy and he uses the performing arts to express himself and to work out any negative energy. If he is stressed or anxious and is unable to move/dance/sing then his behaviour gets quite out of hand. He has always liked bright colours and sparkle and that is combined with being a talented dancer; he has been called 'a girl' at school a number of times - often by the 'sporty' boys. Thankfully his teachers have helped to stamp out name-calling and he has been given an older boy mentor at school now who has walked his path so can give some guidance but it hasn't always been easy, especially at primary school. He has always had huge empathy for others and will show emotion easily (which is actually a great asset for any future career in the performing arts!), but that is not always understood by others when boys are often told 'men don't cry', and that has lead to problems for David with other children.

Reflection points

1. How can I help the sensitive boy experience a sense of belonging which doesn't pressure him to feel that he has to be untrue to who he is? Is there a creative club or friendship group I could help facilitate?
2. Are there names that the sensitive boy has been called that maybe I need to talk about with him? It's important for sensitive boys to hear you speaking positively about them, which can validate and affirm their gifts and strengths and thus dilute the negative names.

Chapter 4

PUTTING ON INVISIBLE ARMOUR OR SHUTTING DOWN

When sensitive children experience rejection, misunderstanding or isolation and the subsequent negative emotions, they can become overwhelmed and need help to process, make sense of and work out what has occurred. Sensitive boys feel things more deeply. When we recognise boys who are sensitive, we can be aware of these experiences hitting them hard and of them feeling these experiences deeply. When we are aware of this tendency we can equip these boys with skills to enable them to excel at life and enjoy being who they are, which will lead to them contributing positively to our society in adulthood.

The feeling of being skinless

This is a phrase that is often used when discussing the feelings of those who are very creative or deep thinkers. Being sensitive or creative can feel raw, as different experiences and environments can cause surprising reactions and emotions to rise up when others seem contrastingly unaffected. 'The term skinlessness seems most appropriate in describing the quality that makes creative artists more susceptible to emotional pain' (Crabtree and Crabtree 2011, p.63).

When these children have an adult who can navigate them through these experiences and put into words some of the possible feelings and reactions, the child can become strong and self aware. But when a sensitive or creative child is raised in an environment where there is little verbal processing of responses, emotions or deep feelings, then the child can become quickly overwhelmed or confused. This can even lead to self loathing or shame, which is discussed further in Chapter 5, or a sense of rejection.

> Skinlessness is best thought of as a hyper-acute sensitivity that can manifest itself in many ways. UK psychologist Gordon Claridge has observed that, 'skinlessless can appear in nightmares, in sensitivity to bodily complaints, and in hyperawareness to sensory stimuli'. (Crabtree and Crabtree 2011, p.63)

Creating an emotional armour

A common way for boys to cope with being sensitive is to develop an 'armour' that protects them from the vulnerability of feeling skinless, deep feelings and being emotional or easily hurt. This armour could be a 'mask', or a persona that they create to hide their real selves behind so that if rejection comes, they feel less rejected as the 'front' that they are using to protect themselves is the part of them that's rejected. They could 'act hard' and be rude or be withdrawn and refuse to speak. They could wear clothes that intimidate others or just look cross. It hurts less when it is these 'fronts' that are being rejected rather than their real self, which may be feeling vulnerable and in turmoil. In the short term they can find it helpful to use these defensive strategies, unless they become so normal that the child forgets that they are using this invisible armour, because then they may find it difficult to become connected again with their real selves. They can feel lost within themselves, confused, a fraud or empty as they continue to present as someone other than themselves. This coping method also causes loneliness because real emotional connection that enables healthy living needs to be authentic and friends who connect to the presenting part of the person rather than the 'real' part of the person are 'useful' but don't feed the emptiness of their soul.

Shutting down

When a person feels misunderstood or scared to be who they are, with all the depth and colour that they feel, then they can end up shutting down. It could start with having to 'wear an emotional armour' to protect themselves but it can end up with them shutting down their creativity, their deep feelings or thoughts, their intuition and any other components of a sensitive boy. The shutdown response can be intentional, but it is usually a slow, subconscious reaction to negativity, which is self-protective. When someone feels emotionally shut down, they can feel:

- angry
- dead inside
- sad
- confused
- lethargic
- frustrated
- numb.

Numb, lethargic or feeling dead inside

These feelings, that are often caused by having to shut down emotionally, can lead a child or adolescent to seek out ways of feeling alive. This can mean that self-harming, drugs or any other adrenaline-releasing, risk-taking experiences could become addictive. Sometimes these children may come across as apathetic or lazy, but have actually 'given up' in some way; however, because it's often a subconscious reaction rather than a considered cognitive one, they may not recognise it themselves. The simplest approach is to help them understand themselves, the way they tick, their talents, experiences and uniqueness which have led them to shut down. Then they can choose to want to unfreeze and become who they really are. Because this state is so rooted in their early experiences of relationships, which lie in their subconscious as implicit memories, some kind of psychotherapy can be really beneficial to unlock the twisted neural pathways of confusion and sadness.

Biddulph describes the common shutting down response that can take place in communities such as schools that don't overtly enable a culture that includes emotional literacy and wellbeing. He describes how boys end up having to shut down feelings such as sadness, disappointment and fear in order to be accepted, and the negative consequences that can follow.

> To make himself cope, a boy hardens his feelings and tenses his body... Boys want to feel alive in their bodies. That's why they like music with a heavy beat, and why they love activity, speed and danger. They instinctively know this can help them break through into manhood. (Biddulph 1995, p.125)

Angry, aggressive and frustrated

When a person feels rejected, misunderstood or socially isolated, they may end up burying deep feelings of anger and frustration. With every unkind word, every angry adult telling them off for not conforming and every experience of confusion about how to process feelings and sensory experiences, it can cause a bucket load of anger or frustration to be poured into their insides.

Eventually these strong feelings can become explosive and the person can seem very prone to emotional reactions that seem disproportionate to the incidents that seemed to trigger them. Sometimes these feelings can be so overwhelming as they bubble away inside them that they have to shut down further, in order to cope and not create further rejection or chaos.

Oaklander, pioneer of Gestalt therapy work with children, argues that anger is an emotion that is often misunderstood and many young boys deny it and push it down, which can be detrimental to their emotional wellbeing (Crenshaw and Stewart 2016, p.219). Oaklander developed a three-phase approach to managing anger and aggression. Phase one described talking about and exploring the angry feelings. Phase two described the important stage of expressing this anger in different creative ways. The third phase explored whether or not there was any buried or unresolved anger due to loss or grief in the subconscious. This last phase has to be approached slowly and gently so that the anger can be released gradually and carefully (Crenshaw and Stewart 2016).

How can a sensitive male come back to life again?

I believe that when a sensitive boy begins to understand themselves and the way that their personality and interests come packaged with challenges in the way society currently relates to them they can begin to build up some resilience to the misunderstanding and negativity they may experience.

I also believe that when they are able to find others who are similar, whether the same age or older, they can feel less strange and less socially isolated. They need to be championed and celebrated as males who are full of life and strength who will be able to contribute something unique and wonderful to the world as they develop.

In an environment of affirmation, positive words and understanding, they will be able to become strong and confident in who they are.

Brown speaks about the power of shame and the way it can cause people to shut down with overwhelm or stress. She describes the difference between women's shame experiences and men's shame experiences and the impact of them:

> As men described their shame experiences to me, I started seeing a very small box. A box that is hammered closed by expectations of always appearing tough, strong, powerful, successful, fearless and in-control and capable. (Brown 2008, p.281)

When boys are shamed for expressing emotion and they subsequently shut down their feelings or dreams or social ease, they can eventually feel that they have already 'lost themselves'. However, when they understand the impact of shame and the implicit society belief system, they can feel empowered to stand up and be counted as strong. Strong enough to express emotion and strong enough to be authentic and not hide and pretend.

When they have adults around them who celebrate them and support them, they can bring change to the culture of their communities and enjoy being accepted as strong, powerful males who have healthy emotions. They can learn to connect emotionally again when they are connected with people who understand and can enjoy their talent, individuality and perception of the world.

Paul's story

Being a creative/sensitive boy growing up had its challenges.

My Year 5 school report said something along the lines of 'Paul often spends time with the girls in his class and they readily accept him'.

I did not choose to spend my free time running about or playing football, which my male peers naturally chose to do and therefore this unfortunately set me apart. This, coupled with my interest in the arts, being creative and performing (especially as a dancer), further removed me from a natural affinity with other boys my age.

However, during secondary education, I increasingly did not enjoy activities that boys are typically associated with – I began to really dislike PE lessons, particularly outdoor games, and hated the environment of the boys' changing rooms. On reflection, I think my feelings and lack of confidence had less to do with the actual sport and more to do with my lack of confidence in all-male environments – I didn't understand the other boys, their attitudes or why they behaved as they did; I think they probably didn't understand me either.

It took me a long time to really identify myself as a 'man'. This does not mean that I ever felt like a girl, female or like a woman at all, it's just that I did not particularly relate to typical male attributes. I definitely felt like a boy and male but struggled to identify myself with an adult idea of manhood, even by the age of 24. On reflection I think this is because I had learnt to reject the attitudes of my male peers in response to their rejection of me - perhaps some might say as self-preservation. Over time and thanks to a significant number of very supportive men - and women - who actively encouraged and accepted me, I have learnt that, although I might not be 'typical', I am no less of a man. In fact, I have learnt that my atypical embodiment of manhood is actually a strength and allows me to bring something different to the party.

Reflection points

1. What behaviour is the sensitive boy displaying that may show they are struggling?
2. Do they feel valued and understood, or do they need help from a mentor or creative therapist to process some of the turmoil they have felt and experienced?

Chapter 5

OUR SUBCONSCIOUS AND THE IMPACT OF BULLYING

Each child arrives in the world with unique fingerprints, and a unique combination of strengths and weaknesses and a unique setting for these to develop in. Strangely, our society seems to encourage people to conform to expectations that are often set in the media. Peer pressure and 'group think' continue to gather pace as individuality is often viewed as a threat or confusing. Yet when people have to conform, sometimes a little part of them can feel starved or ignored. We need to be intentional about celebrating children's strengths and giving language to articulate weakness as normal, with the potential to become a strength or the flip side of a specific strength.

Parent pressure and expectation

One tendency in our society is for parents to repeatedly refer to their children as similar to themselves, which can hinder their ability to become who they are. They can feel limited and confined by the expectations and fail to flourish in their individuality if they are looked on as a 'mini me' of the parents. When a child is encouraged to be someone whom the parent wants them to be, the consequence is that the child can feel rejected for who they really are. They can internalise a sense of disappointment or even shame for not being who they were 'meant to be' and can reject themselves. Putting pressure on a child to excel at things that they may not be keen on can be deeply damaging and cause the same consequences as if the child was rejected explicitly. Yet we do see it happen subtly all the time!

It is important to support children and adolescents as they discover who they are and what they themselves feel passionate about. Discovering who we are is a life-long process but is especially important in childhood and early adolescence. Helping a child dream about their future is an important part of childhood.

The impact of early years

All babies are emotionally driven, particularly in their first two years of life, and store all their emotional experiences and interactions in the right hemisphere of the brain. For boys especially, it seems that as their left brain (logical, analytical, verbal) begins to become more dominant, they learn to behave in a way that gets the most rewards despite their early right brain experiences, and a conflict arises. At this stage, primary caregivers can become aware that boys will then often become more restricted in their emotional understanding and practice of empathy and will often begin to value aggression or competitiveness as hallmarks of masculinity, which can conflict with their first two years' experience of life.

> Later in their development, the influence of socialisation experiences with peers, parents, teachers, media images become prominent. These forces deemphasise right brain skills such as empathising, reflecting on one's inner life... (Kiselica, Englar-Carson and Horne 2008, p.11)

Therefore it is worth noting that to enable a sensitive boy to develop confidently and happily in our current communities, we need to be mindful about speaking positively about sensitive boys and also be aware that such an approach can go against much of society's understanding of masculine and male.

The threat response and the consequences of feeling fear

> Never underestimate the impact of childhood bullying on the brains, minds and hearts of your clients... Most incidents of bullying are public displays witnessed and remembered by others in the service of establishing or maintaining social hierarchy. (Cozolino 2016, p.144)

When a child is repeatedly teased, bullied, socially rejected, feels overwhelmed or frightened and is not able to process the experience, it can be traumatic. The fact is that our bodies respond to trauma essentially by setting off alarms internally that enable us to run away or freeze as a response to the threat. This is meant to help us to survive, but, when someone has been repeatedly scared or emotionally overwhelmed when they are little and dependent on adults to meet their needs, and they don't get their survival brain soothed and calmed, they begin to develop a brain that is almost always wired on hyper-alert because the world seems to be so scary.

This 'threat response' is important to understand because it helps children know that when they have a physical and emotional response to trauma, they are not being naughty or strange but responding in a way that is expected. As adults, our response is the same!

It is good to remember that, when any of us feel threatened, we naturally respond with this 'fight, flight or freeze' response, usually without noticing it.

So, let's unpack this response a bit so that we can see how it affects us and children who have been traumatised. The 'fight, flight or freeze' response is sometimes called the 'threat response' and it is based in our brainstem, which is the area of the brain near the back of the neck. This is where our most basic responses, like breathing and heart rate, are based. In fact, it's the only area of the brain that is fully formed when a baby is born.

This area is linked to another area in the brain called the 'limbic system,' which, if faced with something it feels is a threat, makes our emotions respond with panic. Doing so releases hormones to prepare and enable our bodies to run (flight), hide (freeze) or scream loudly or physically fight (fight).

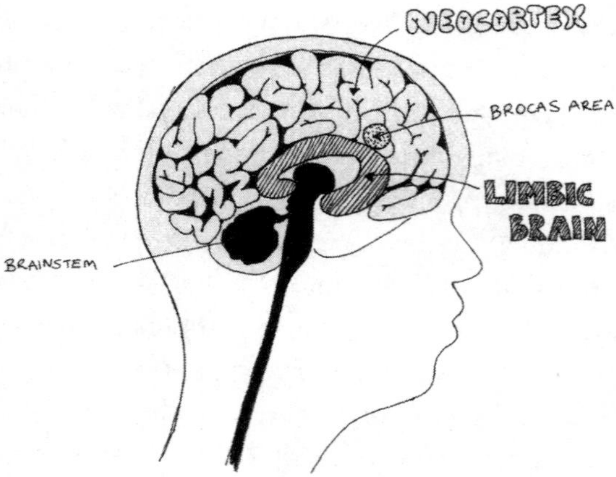

Meanwhile, when this threat response happens, the ability to think, be rational, negotiate or reflect goes offline. The rational part of the brain is the front part and is called the 'pre-frontal cortex'; there is reduced neural activity in this area of the brain when someone feels threat or fear which causes emotional and subconscious responses to events.

The other area of the brain that goes 'offline' when we feel threatened is the 'brocas' area which is responsible for speech and language. That's why it can be really difficult to express how we feel in words when we've just experienced something really awful, and why children often look shocked and wide-eyed and say nothing when they are shouted at.

If the traumatic experience happens repeatedly then it would be normal for the child to live in a continual state of threat. This then makes it really difficult for the child to think, reason, negotiate or reflect, as that part of the brain is not working well due to the amount of stress hormones pumping around the child's body and the feelings of terror that are dominating the child's internal world. This is called the 'prolonged threat response' because the brain gets stuck in a response to possible threat all the time.

Helping a child recover from fear

So, to sum up, the threat response impacts on a child's behaviour, their feelings and their relationships because they don't feel safe, but instead feel threatened, scared, confused and unstable.

There is more about the impact of experiencing terror and powerlessness in my book, *The Simple Guide to Child Trauma* (2016).

The only way to enable a child to recover is to help them feel calm and safe by being a safe person that can support and help them; this enables the threat response to be reduced and the cognitive pre-frontal cortex to come back online and make good decisions. It's important for a sensitive boy to know that when they have a threat response, they are not being naughty, but are responding to feeling really terrified. They don't need discipline or labelling but they do need support to become calm.

Our subconscious responses

Most of us acknowledge that the majority of our responses and reactions come from our subconscious, not from the cognitive part of our brain. Many of our experiences, especially the ones that are negative, are stored in our subconscious alongside the implicit decisions that have subsequently followed to intentionally avoid re-experiencing the same horrific feelings of fear, powerlessness or shame. The aim of psychotherapy is to begin to unpack some of this subconscious so that it has less power on our reactions and to provide an opportunity to use the frontal lobes to process, think through and reflect on our responses. All early childhood experiences of rejection, bullying, abuse, fear, being abandoned, wanting emotional connection with a caregiver, needing to vocalise a need but being unable to, and other such childhood traumas, are held in the part of the brain where implicit memories lie. This is why cognitive approaches which focus on changing behaviour that is driven by deep subconscious memories are often unhelpful and can actually cause an increase in shame and shame-based behaviours.

Seigel and Bryson explain the importance of enabling children to express their feelings and helping them to take time to process and talk about their experiences. They explain that if children are not offered that opportunity they can struggle to make sense of what has happened, which can be negative in the short and longer term.

> But when we help our kids integrate their past into their present, they can make sense of what's going on inside them and gain control over how they think and behave. The more you promote this type of memory integration in your child, the less often you will see irrational responses to what's happening now that are really left over reactions from the past. (Siegel and Payne Bryson 2012, p.78)

The power of shame

When I am delivering training, I ask those attending to become 'shame police' – to quickly stop shame being used in any setting to assert power over vulnerable children and young people and to protect them from the excruciating experience of shame. It's important to recognise the power and pain that shame brings. It's hard to describe the level of pain because it feels so awful and the natural response is powerful and usually linked with a desire to run away, hide or in some way escape the pain.

When a child feels shame, whether because they were teased or they couldn't answer a question or they did something embarrassing in public and people laughed, they feel a deep internal experience of hating themselves.

> Shame is that feeling in the pit of your stomach that is dark and hurts like hell. (Brown 2008, p.4)

There is a huge difference between shame, embarrassment, humiliation and guilt. Embarrassment should only last a while and can usually be something that can be laughed about after a while. Humiliation is usually about another person trying to cause embarrassment to a person and is not a nice experience, which causes a rupture in a relationship due to unpleasant motives from the person intending to cause the humiliation. Guilt is an emotion that indicates that a person has done something wrong but has the power to put it right or say sorry, after which the emotion can then subside. Shame is a feeling that causes the person to feel that the very core of who they are is bad, not what they have done or said, but who they are. When someone feels shame, it can cause the same neurological response as the threat response. Think of something just awful happening to you, like standing up to deliver a presentation and freezing and having no words. Usually, such a response would mean that the person could struggle to think, be reasonable, rational or access creative words to express themselves and other reactions that are dependent on the pre-frontal cortex. This causes an increase in anxiety and the shame lodges in the subconscious as an implicit memory that informs and dictates behaviour to avoid re-experiencing the emotion.

Bullying can cause deep shame

Bullying can cause deep shame. The bullied boys may feel like they are the 'loser', the 'useless one', the 'reject' and so recoil internally and begin to believe the feeling. This creates a sense of self-loathing and internal turmoil, which can escalate with every further experience of shame-driven bullying. Other initiation rites that are experienced in groups of boys can also cause huge implicit wells of shame to form as peers ridicule, humiliate and taunt the victim. This abuse can cause a deep sense of powerlessness, self-hatred and anger to reside in the subconscious, influencing behaviour so as to avoid having to ever succumb to such terror again.

When a child can speak to a warm, kind adult about their experiences, they are more likely to be able to unpack the poisonous toxins of the shame that is held internally and begin to be free from its influence over emotions, behaviour, relationships and decisions.

> When we are honest about our struggles, we are much less likely to get stuck in shame. This is critical because shame diminishes our capacity to practice empathy. (Brown 2008, p.59)

As adults, let's make sure we notice the tiny signs and stop all bullying, teasing, mocking, name-calling, humiliating and any unkind initiations that still exist. You can restore a child's dignity and reduce the shame quickly by stopping it, distracting the other children and then identifying with the victim in some way by telling a quick story of how you once 'got caught in that situation' or 'fell over' or whatever has caused the shame to be felt.

Jon's story

I loved school and didn't find it too hard because I was seen as a musician, and that label protected me from having to 'fit in'. I did see some of my friends trying to prove their manhood when they became teenagers and felt devastated that they had to do things they knew they didn't want to do - just so they could feel like they could fit in. I just kept myself busy with performances which were adrenaline-rich experiences instead.

Reflection points

1. Have I noticed that my sensitive boy has had a 'threat response' and struggled to think clearly? Does the sensitive boy find that in any specific context? Does he express his feelings of fear or nervousness or has he become shut down and silent about feelings of fear?
2. Who speaks positively to him about his skills and strengths? Can I encourage other adults to speak out about his positive qualities, as this will build resilience and courage?

Chapter 6

RELATIONSHIPS THAT CREATE RESILIENCE

We know that, for children and adolescents, relationships are the catalyst for recovery from the impact of negative experiences in life. Relationships can also enable a sensitive boy to develop resilience so he can flourish in a world that doesn't always understand or seem to care.

Attachment and attunement

A child is born relationally wired with a desire to attach to his or her primary caregiver(s), no matter who that person is, or how they may feel about the new arrival. This first relational attachment is designed to become the foundation of their sense of self, from which stem confidence and self-worth. When a child experiences consistent love, nurture and care, he or she then believes that they are worth that attention and is consequently able to trust others. It is now becoming widely accepted that the first five years of a child's life is the primary time in which the brain develops most significantly.

Healthy infant development is all about the caregiver's 'attunement' or careful 'tuning in' to the baby's needs, and how the baby perceives the world as friendly or hostile depending on the quality of these earliest interactions.

When a parent is attuned to a child and their needs, the child feels safe, stable, known, loved, connected and therefore secure in that moment. 'The child's internal world is seen with clarity by the parent and the parent comes to resonate with the child's state' (Siegel 2007, p.27). When this experience is repeated consistently, it actually develops the regulatory circuits in the brain (the pre-frontal cortex or thinking brain at the front). This creates resilience and an ability to continue to be self-regulated, reflective, calm and resilient. The continual experience of being attuned to also enables children to become naturally empathetic to others.

This early experience of attachment begins in the womb and enables a child to form a 'secure base' from which to explore the world (Bowlby 2006). A newborn baby will cry and screw up their little face until the mother begins to soothe and provide comfort; the baby responds with relief and the mother also sighs with relief. A father will gaze into his baby's eyes with love and wonder, and a baby will respond with coos and eyes that shine with delight in the repetitive, relational experience. The 'dance' between these two or three participants continues as a baby's needs are met, and a baby's brain forms neural pathways that then expect warm, genuine, kind and loving relationships.

The practice of responding to the emotional cues of a child is called being 'attuned' to them and their needs.

When a baby cries there is increased neural activity in both the baby's and the mother's brains, which lead to the connection response. This reciprocal response is the very essence of the positive attachment behaviour pattern between a baby and a parent, and consequently the neurons involved have been called 'mirror neurons', first identified by Giamcomo Rizzolatti in the early 1990s (see Rizzolatti and Sinigaglia 2008). This has helped us to understand how humans can feel another person's feelings and respond accordingly: when a baby sees another baby cry, they often cry too; when a parent feeds their baby, they often open their mouths as their baby opens their mouth to be fed; and when someone sees a chair fall from a table onto someone else's head, it is not unusual to see them also wince as if the chair was going to harm them too.

The dance of relationship that develops healthy children

It is this process of attuned responding that establishes a reciprocal expectation system that then enables a child to learn emotional self-regulation during the early stages of development and to carry this through into adulthood.

A child learns to regulate their psychological arousal because of the presence of this familiar attachment figure, who is able to respond in a repetitive and predictable way by either comforting or stimulating as needed. When an attachment figure is able to soothe the little one, it not only enables comfort at that particular moment, but it also enables the formation of a biological framework for dealing with future stress or need. The repetitive action of soothing and comforting a child when they are distressed is called co-regulation and eventually enables the child to develop their own ability to calm themselves down, self-soothe and have an internal sense of security, thus creating emotional resilience. If a child doesn't have exposure to this attachment relationship of predictable, repetitive, calming, and soothing behaviour which co-regulates with them, they will struggle to learn to self-regulate their emotions and will present with behaviour that reflects this.

This primary attachment relationship hopefully remains with a child as they grow older and, importantly, it also enables them to develop other attachment relationships.

Emotional connection

Not only is this primary attachment figure the 'safe base' for a child because they are the source of safety and comfort, but it is also within this attachment relationship that a child first learns emotional literacy. As the caregiver responds to a child's needs and feelings, they are also able to provide words to them. For example, if a child was crying after falling over, a parent might comfort them and say, 'Oh dear, it can feel so scary when you hurt yourself, can't it? I am wondering if you feel sad or scared or upset right now?' This then builds the child's capacity for reflective thinking and helps them to explore different words for different feelings.

> Putting feelings into words has long served a positive function for many individuals suffering from stress and trauma. Even writing about your experiences supports top-down modulation of emotion and bodily responses. (Cozolino 2016, p.24)

When a child has not had these repetitive experiences in early childhood, they can find it strange and challenging to be asked to reflect on or name any feelings that they may be experiencing. They will be unfamiliar with managing strong emotions and they may feel fear of how powerless they are in the face of such strong emotional responses. This uncertainty and inability to reflect upon or understand familiar feelings can lead to children using behaviours, rather than words, to express their feelings. This can then lead to difficult relational experiences due to these expressions of strong feelings, which in turn can reinforce the fear and lack of trust within relationships. For a child already in a negative relational behaviour pattern, this will continue into adulthood unless there is a person who provides a positive, consistent, predictable relationship, and spends time helping the child to learn these vital skills.

When a child experiences a repetitive negative response to their expression of need or feelings, then they will learn to survive with different coping mechanisms, many of which can be quite difficult for them or for the other people around them.

If a child experiences caring, relational interactions that are continually repeated and repeated, then they are able to trust that relational process and consequently have the emotional resilience to explore more relationships and new situations.

Resilience is primarily actually created when children experience some degree of stress, but the fear or anxiety that they feel is then relieved due to the presence of a comforting, reassuring, secure adult. When a child experiences stress without such an adult being present, then they are aroused but with no skill-set available to be able to recover easily or manage their strong emotions.

Empathy and kindness

The foundation of a relationship that enables a child to grow and develop healthily is one that recognises the value of empathy and kindness. It sounds simple, but children can be really irritating and can enjoy winding us up just to see how we react! But when they are continually met with patience, kindness or empathy rather than anger, frustration and lack of patience, they themselves learn to be people who demonstrate such qualities. If they don't experience kindness and patience, they will find it hard to give to others. When things do go wrong and impatience, irritation and frustration become the dominant emotions expressed, it is important to have created a culture where both adults and children say sorry naturally. This can be very healing and healthy as a template for future relationships.

Mis-attunement

When a parent wants a child to be someone who is like them or good at something they are good at or wanted to be good at, the child can experience mis-attunement. This can feel like rejection to the child and the impact of such a relationship on the child can be distressing. This seems to happen when a child who is sensitive or creative has a father who believes, for example, that the highest value of masculinity is expressed as strength and sports ability. The sensitive son is left knowing he can never please his father or be the person his father really wants to have relationship with.

This rejection can be catastrophic to the child's healthy emotional development. When a child is frequently misunderstood by a primary caregiver, it can lead to alienation and confusion.

Cozolino (2016) describes how traumatising it can be for children when their primary caregivers are misattuned or emotionally unavailable:

> It appears that experiences of emotional misattunment with parents trigger the same parasympathetic reflex as being scolded or abandoned. Thus the emotional unavailability of the parent is experienced as a rejection and interpreted as, 'I'm not important, valuable or lovable enough to be secure in my membership in the family' – which feels life threatening when survival depends upon your family's protection. These experiences may occur in early attachment relationships when an

> excited expectation of connection in a child is met with inattention, indifference or anger from a parent or caregiver. (Cozolino 2016, p.121)

When a sensitive child is navigating himself through life, he can be easily overwhelmed by experiences that others may find normal. This can cause a 'clash' relationally unless there is an approach that is curious rather than furious, and that is accepting of the different ways we can all view life. For example, if a young boy is moved to tears by a film, an argument, a sad looking person, a piece of art on a wall, the sound of an instrument or any other experience, he need an adult to help him understand what's going on. He needs the following:

1. validation of the emotion (rather than laughing, devaluing or questioning)
2. empathy with the impact it has had on him (nurture, care and love)
3. an opportunity to reflect on words that could be used to describe the reaction or experience (to enable self-regulation of the strong emotions).

If this suggested response takes place in the context of a warm, nurturing, protective relationship then the child won't feel shamed, weird, confused, hurt or in turmoil, but will be able to grow in confidence and ability to self-regulate.

Roger's story

My Dad wanted a football player and I felt like I was a disappointment to him my whole life. I tried to please him and show interest but I felt like I wasn't allowed to be who I felt I was and so it felt like a huge wall came between us. That made me feel increasingly anxious and often depressed. It was only as an adult I felt able to explore my masculinity and feel peace that actually I was OK just as I was.

Reflection points

1. What attachment relationship does this sensitive boy have?
2. How much does he enjoy the relief of an attuned relationship or how much does he feel the turmoil of a mis-attuned relationship where he actually feels rejected?
3. Could you help the adults in his world explore this and put into words an apology and then start celebrating the sensitive boy with words and actions?

Chapter 7

MANAGING FEAR AND WORRY

Children are prone to worrying about things that they don't understand. They like to overhear conversations to see if they can make more sense out of life, but in the process can misunderstand a lot of things, which can cause anxiety. I have found after two decades of parenting that they hear more than we think and notice, and can read more than we can realise in their eagerness to interact with their worlds. The problem is that they don't always show the adults around them when they have misunderstood things or are worried about things. This can be because they feel bad that they heard things they know they weren't meant to, and so feel awkward asking for clarification or comfort. It could be that they misunderstand and reach conclusions that cause them to be fearful, or withdraw from their relationships. Little boys can often speak confidently to the adults around them about how they weren't negatively affected and were in fact amused by what they have heard, when in fact this is a coping mechanism to hide the shame and turmoil that they experienced.

Ultimately, they need to have a relationship with an adult where they can ask the questions that bother them and make sense of their world in an age-appropriate way.

Protecting sensitive boys

I believe that every issue needs to be addressed differently at every age during childhood. For example, for a small child to have a description of the process of reproduction in exact detail can be terrifying and as such it needs to be adapted as they grow older and can understand more. For a child to understand the huge world issues around poverty and injustice can create a terrifying world for a child that hinders their ability to grow confidently and innocently. This is not us protecting them from the reality and therefore overprotecting them, but recognising that knowledge needs to be age-appropriate for them to be able to grapple with the issues and not have to use unhelpful coping mechanisms to manage the information that they have been given.

I fully believe that when a child is not yet in adolescence, they need to have a relatively innocent view of the world, so that whatever they do know about what is not right, they hold a view that their parents and other such adults can 'fix it' and so they don't have to worry. The reality of world issues and adult topics needs to be carefully unfolded according to the age and the emotional development of the child.

The weight of the world

When a sensitive child is not able to emotionally connect with an adult who is meant to be helping them navigate their emotional world, they can sometimes end up feeling like they carry the weight of the world on their shoulders. Children are meant to have a freedom that is harder to achieve in adulthood, because they should be able to be innocent and protected from intense worrying by the adults who care for them. When children worry a lot, they can sometimes end up taking the role of an adult in a relationship, where they care for their caregiver and discuss the adult's concerns and anxieties. When a child ends up engaging in adult discussion and cares, they lose their ability to be carefree and innocent and carry emotional weight that is too big for a child to carry. This unhelpful and dysfunctional 'parenting of the parent' can occur naturally when sensitive children are parented by someone who is struggling with challenges such as mental illness or a difficult, volatile relationship. It can happen when a sibling or parent is seriously ill and the child feels that they have to be the primary comfort for the other relatives. It is important that the child does not end up focusing on caring for the parent but is able to stay the child in the relationship and be free to play innocently. Children shouldn't take responsibility for their siblings, for finance, for their parents' health, for their parents' marriage, for the provision of food or drink in the home, but instead should be able to assume that the grown-ups will take care of those issues.

Sensitive children and siblings

It can be really difficult raising sensitive children when there are other siblings around who are less sensitive or older in age, and therefore interested in subjects that are not suitable for the younger or more sensitive children. Discussion around the meal table can be tricky and consideration is needed regarding what is on any television or radio in a family room, if the subject matter could be inappropriate or unhelpful for the younger or more sensitive child. It can seem to take too much time and effort to protect these children from media that is unsuitable, but it is worth the effort because one age-inappropriate image without context could really impact a child in the long term.

When a child is exposed to too much information about the world and issues which ought to be the sole concern of adults, the child can become overwhelmed and that will present in behaviours that can look like they are angry or naughty, whereas actually they are anxious and scared.

Help with boundaries

By nature, sensitive boys are likely to be nurturers and feel deeply, and as such we need to be aware that they need us as adults to help them to process the feelings that have impacted them, but also, and most importantly, they need us to help them learn to set boundaries. They need to know that they are not responsible for the world's happiness. They are not even responsible for anyone else's happiness and they need to learn that they must not look after others' needs while ignoring their own. They need to hear that it's OK to put themselves first and that setting boundaries does not make them selfish.

Understanding their own sensitivities

If a sensitive boy is too protected or if the adults around them clearly display signs of anxiety themselves about their child's welfare, the child can become stifled and this can eventually lead to them feeling like they are numb inside. It is important for boys to take risks, to try new things, to fail, to fall over and hurt themselves and learn how to self-regulate their emotions. Once they have had an adult helping them to respond to their emotions or overwhelm, preferably in the first few years of life, the aim is for the child to learn to use those tools that they need.

We are all different, and we need time to reflect and to explore and understand these differences. I know that I can't watch films with too much terror in them. I am visually very impacted and therefore I have to be careful what I watch. I know the negative impact can be disruptive and so I know it's worth me having that boundary. Children need to process the negative impact that has occurred when they have seen something, heard something, been somewhere or been with certain people or any other experience that can cause emotional turmoil, so that they can understand themselves better. What they don't need or want is for the parent or carer to continually monitor or control what they do and display their own anxiety about the child becoming anxious! Anxiety is catching! When a parent is anxious about something, it can cause the children and other people around them to be anxious about the same thing. Sensitive boys need the adults in their world to help them trust themselves and help them know that they will be OK, they can fail and pick themselves up again, they can be hurt but recover, and they are stronger than they think.

The importance of not over-protecting a child

Obviously when parenting or helping a sensitive boy, it can be natural to want to protect, comfort and help the child avoid difficulties or challenge. You may know that when they struggle they can become overwhelmed or deeply sad and so it is natural to try and avoid that happening. The problem is that they will only become strong when they are able to choose to do things that challenge them, and have time to make mistakes, overcome fear, reflect, recover and celebrate. This is a tricky balance and not easy to get right, but the aim is for boys to feel empowered to challenge themselves, take risks and push themselves out of their comfort zones and yet know that they have adults who are emotionally supportive and who they can process their feelings with.

It is important for a child to sometimes play alone and not have to tell the adults what they were doing. It is important for them to challenge themselves physically and for the adults to be calm and reflective about the risks but not stop them (unless it's an obvious danger!).

It is important that sensitive boys do not end up with a label on them that constricts the possibilities for them, but instead empowers them to go beyond what they thought they could achieve.

Sam's story

I grew up as invisible as possible due to my mum being poorly. She was mentally ill and so the house was wired to being about her needs, so I learned quickly to just get on with things. I did see and hear things that would keep me awake for years as I tried to understand them. Things that kids shouldn't see. I always wondered why my mates would love to watch stuff on TV that freaked me out and I had to pretend I loved it - but I wasn't OK.

Images would seem to imprint on my mind and I never had anyone to help me know my boundaries. I felt the weight of the world on my shoulders and still struggle now with feeling like everything is my responsibility.

Reflection points

1. Do you think your sensitive boy has been exposed to stimulation that has been unhelpful for his age and sensitivity?
2. Do you think he has become overwhelmed with too much information and visual and sensory information?
3. Does he seem to carry the weight of the world on his shoulders? Can you speak to him about his worries and support him?

Chapter 8

WHAT DOES ANXIETY LOOK LIKE IN CHILDREN?

Sensitive children can experience a lot of anxiety and yet can often be unable to use words to describe it to others, which can lead to increased fear because they are uncertain what is going in internally. Therefore, it is important to be able to reflect with a child on their feelings and body sensations. What do they feel emotionally? What can they feel in their body?

They could experience the following physical sensations that could be a sign of anxiety:

- headaches, dizziness, restlessness, sleep interruptions, nightmares
- difficulty swallowing, dry mouth, constant coughing
- difficulty breathing, chest pain, palpitations
- nausea, cramping, tummy aches, diarrhoea
- picking skin, hair pulling.

They could feel and show the following behaviours:

- agitation and restlessness
- anger with emotional outbursts, where they feel out of control

- lack of confidence and wanting to 'hide' or feeling lethargic
- worried with negative thought patterns going round their heads.

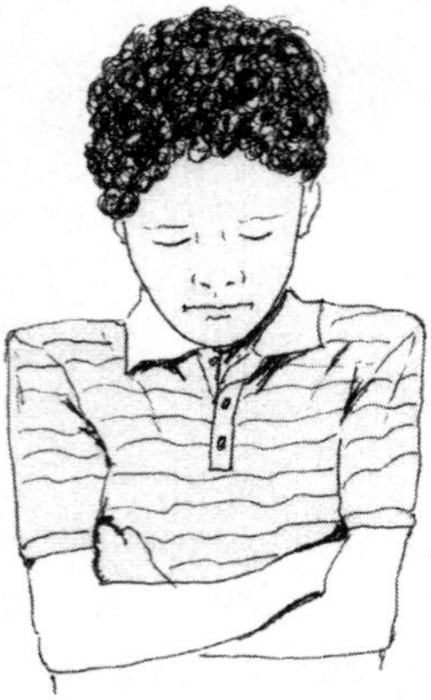

Although the physical symptoms could be due to a whole host of other medical reasons (and therefore do be sensible about always consulting with medical professionals), they could also be signs of anxiety. It may become apparent if the physical symptoms were due to anxiety when the child is helped to reflect calmly and slowly on what is going on for them internally and can pinpoint some reasons. What first caused them to feel that way? Has it happened before? What did they do last time that helped? Anxiety can often be relieved when they understand what normal physiological symptoms are, such as butterflies in their tummy when they are going to do a performance, or feeling sick when they are going to sit a test. When these things can be discussed and the adult is able to refer to little stories of when they experienced the same kind of responses, the child is able to feel less afraid of their anxiety and this can reduce the symptoms.

Ways to reduce anxiety

- Teach children that worrying is normal and take time to explain to them what happens to their brain and body when they worry. The more the child understands what is happening, the less they become anxious about the anxiety.
- Remember an event or time when you were anxious and tell the story of how you felt, what happened and how you felt afterwards. Then walk through the thing they are frightened about, using words but also talking about emotions and how they can affect your body. This helps the right hemisphere of the brain, which can feel otherwise feel overwhelmed, to be less reactive and enables the child to feel more integrated and prepared.
- Breathing exercises can help a child calm down and be able to reflect again. They can also help a child to stop worrying about the 'what ifs' and instead be more present in the here and now.
- Create mini goals in areas where there is anxiety. Rather than avoiding the thing that causes the anxiety, it's good to focus on aims to achieve

something that is a step towards the ultimate goal of not being fearful. Celebrating every step is important!

- Let them have a reminder of you or someone they love with them at all times which is age-appropriate. If they are older they can have something small in their pocket or a favourite photo on their phone or something that smells reassuring on them. When they are younger they can have a favourite cuddly toy or fidget toy in their pocket or bag that they can go and use to comfort themselves.
- It can be helpful to describe to the child the anxiety as a wave to surf and then breathe deeply until the peaks get smaller and smaller.
- Make sure that they are sleeping well and exercising, as both of these can reduce anxiety significantly.
- Distraction can work in the short term as long as they are helped to reflect on the anxiety afterwards. They may like to picture a safe place where they feel calm.
- Try stretching or pushing against a wall. Tensing muscles and then relaxing them again can help relax the child. It's good to push or stretch for 10 seconds and then relax for 10 and repeat.

Self-regulation activities

It is important to create a culture where adults model reflection and self-regulation. It is good for adults to reflect on their own emotions with words like, 'I am thinking that I feel grumpy today. I wonder why that is? Maybe I didn't get enough sleep. Or am I worried about how to get through my pile of work. Now what can I do? Maybe some deep breathing?'

It can also be helpful for adults to model breathing exercises and other useful ways of calming down and relaxing, such as drawing, exercises and getting out a special sensory or comfortable thing.

There are other self-regulation activities that can be found in my book *The Simple Guide to Child Trauma* (2016).

Helping children to understand emotions

When children live in an environment where emotions are not verbally explored and not expressed without a sense of nervousness, the child can learn that emotions are to be hidden and denied. This can lead to internalisation, which can lead to inner turmoil and frozen emotions.

Children need to learn how to express feelings at an early age and in a way that is appropriate and helpful. Young children will always start off their lives expressing feelings naturally but will change their expressions according to the way they are received and understood. Children who repress or inhibit emotions are taught to do so as a result of negative reactions to their expression of feelings. This negative experience of expressing emotion that is not met with empathy and understanding can lead to confusion, fear and feelings of shame. Children will express feelings through behaviour and facial expression and they become 'emotionally literate' when they are older, but only if this behaviour is modelled to them by a caring adult.

> Some children learn to inhibit feelings, most commonly anger, at such a young age that they have no memory of ever feeling them, no words with which to describe them, no skills with which to express them. These children have concluded early on that they are shameful beings. (Oaklander 2007, p.144)

When we help a child to name the emotion that is being felt, it can actually enable them to become calmer. Dan Siegel (2007) suggests that we encourage children to 'name it to tame it'. He suggests that when big emotions are being expressed, it works well to help them tell the story of what is upsetting them. This means that they have to use other parts of their brain, which can help them make sense of their experience and feel less powerless.

How to discipline a sensitive child

First, it is important to remember that discipline actually means 'to teach' and does not mean 'to punish' and as such should be a part of an empathetic, kind, nurturing experience. Cozolino says, 'a disciple is a student, not a recipient of behavioural consequences' (2016, p.139).

- Avoid shaming them with words like 'why can't you be normal'; 'you are so stupid'; 'stop being so highly sensitive, it's exhausting'. Also avoid these words being used to tease the child for being sensitive. Words like that can hurt and cause shame and frustration for being sensitive rather than build up the child's self confidence.
- When a child is sensitive they can find it extremely frightening to be disciplined by social isolation or having 'time out'. They are often not sure how to process the withdrawal of love and care and can feel very unsafe and fearful.
- They also mustn't feel that they can 'get away with anything', as the lack of boundaries can feel very unsafe. Children want to feel powerful but need adults around them to hold clear boundaries so that the child is not powerless, but also doesn't have more power than the adult.

Helpful ways to discipline a sensitive child

1. Connect with the child emotionally before you try and explain any boundary or appropriate behaviour. When a child feels calm and emotionally connected, they often want to learn and can think and reflect.
2. Use body language and tone of voice to connect. Maybe bend down so that you can be their height,

or touch their shoulder lightly and look at them with kindness rather than anger. Use a calm tone of voice and not a frustrated one.

3. Reassure them that you know they are a good kid and don't want to be annoying or naughty, but they obviously misunderstood or got frightened. When a child feels that we respect them and trust them, they usually want to work with us not against us.
4. I quite like asking the child what they think they should do next and reflect with them on that issue. I have found that they may suggest some punitive consequences and I enjoy exploring how I think that may be too harsh and that forgiveness can be enough.

Perfectionism

It's important to be aware that sensitive children can be prone to perfectionism and can feel anxious about failure or anything that isn't how they want it. It is not unusual to see a creative child screwing up their picture whilst announcing tearfully how bad it is. Wanting things to go well and avoiding failure, rejection or disappointment is not unusual for sensitive children and they need support in processing those negative, tough feelings and experiences carefully until they feel less fear. It is hard work supporting them due to the strength of feelings that can be expressed, but it is worth it in the long run to help them live a life less confined by fear.

Callum's story

I thought there was something wrong with me because I often felt sick, dizzy or tearful about anything new or challenging. I hated failing and so would do anything to avoid it. Once I was taught what anxiety was and some ways of coping with it, I felt I was going to be OK again.

Reflection points

1. Does your sensitive boy recognise anxiety and struggle with it?
2. Does he know some strategies he can use to help him?
3. Who does he talk to about his feelings?

Chapter 9

BELIEVING THE BEST ABOUT CHILDREN

A child needs someone in their life to believe in them. They need to learn to believe that they have a purpose, are capable and can offer something of value to society. When they don't have a parent to do that, a teacher or mentor can become that influential person who champions them to become the best that they can be, but they need one adult who can champion them.

Reflecting on how the sensitive boy is doing emotionally

Sometimes it can be hard to assess how children are doing emotionally. There are some clear indications of when things are going wrong and when a child is unhappy, but worried parents can worry the children and over-analysing can be damaging. Here is a helpful list to enable parents, professionals and others to grasp a quick sense of how a child is developing. Perry (2002) suggests that there are clear developmental outcomes that serve as a guideline to informally reflect on psychosocial growth. He speaks of areas that we have explored in this simple guide and suggests that attachment relationships leading to self-regulation behaviour are the foundational experience and subsequent behaviour. He suggests that affiliation – the sense of belonging and then the ability to attune to others and value them – is a sign of emotional health. He then suggests that children and young people should show an ability first to tolerate differences and then ultimately to respect those who are different.

For any of us working or living with sensitive boys or any children, when we can facilitate growth in any of these areas, we are enabling them to grow into healthy adults who can enjoy positive relationships with others.

Emotional connection

Sensitive boys need to know that they are believed in and that we value their gifts and can recognise that the flip side of these strengths can be the vulnerability to become anxious, or overwhelmed, or exhausted, or shut down or numb.

When we communicate with emotional connection that we care and want to support them and want to help them navigate their journey to becoming the best that they can be, then they can become strong and confident.

Confidence versus arrogance

Children and young people can sometimes come across as arrogant, but adults must remember not to be harsh or feel the need to 'take them down a peg or two'. It is not 'our job' to make sure they know how little they know and push them down, shame them, laugh at them or make sure we tell them what they will learn one day. These responses can be significantly damaging. They have their whole lives ahead, which will be full of challenge and difficulty, as well as victory and triumph, and our primary concern is that we have helped them to develop the resources they need to face both.

Our mission to change society for the better

As a society, we need to be proactively fighting for the sensitive boys among us to be celebrated as strongly masculine and powerful. We must recognise their significant value to society as people offering emotional strength and intuition in a society where there are not enough fathers and male role models to help children develop strong self esteem. Let us all use our voices to speak up for males of every shape and size, who have every strength and gift, and let's stop labelling or limiting the possibilities of who they can be. Let us be loud voices who challenge the shallow thinking, and the established or damaging culture around men that has been detrimental for so long.

It has become increasingly apparent in research and then in the media that males struggle with depression and anxiety but are less likely to seek help than females. They often don't have the same ease when speaking about deep issues or things that make them feel vulnerable and this can increase the severity of the challenges they can face. There is increasing evidence that suicide in males is more prevalent than in females. In 2013, 6233 suicides were recorded in the UK for people aged 15 and older. Of these, 78 per cent were male and 22 per cent were female (Bromley *et al.* 2014). Teaching males emotional literacy, prioritising the building of strong emotional connections with parents of males and facilitating a sense of belonging and sense of self can significantly reduce the possibility of intense turmoil to the point of wanting to not live anymore.

Remember that each one of us can make a huge difference. Every word we speak, every time we encourage, every time we use our voice to defend and protect, we are building a community of people who respect and care for each other.

REFERENCES AND RECOMMENDED READING

References

Biddulph, S. (1995) *Raising Boys: Why Boys are Different – How to Help them Become Happy and Well-Balanced Men.* London: Thorsons-Harper Collins.

Bowlby, J (2006) *A Secure Base.* London: Routledge.

Bromley, C. *et al.* (2014) 'The Scottish Health Survey: 2013 edition, volume 1, main report.' Edinburgh: The Scottish Government. Available at www.gov.scot/Resource/0046/00464858.pdf, accessed on 25 August 2017.

Brown, B. (2008) *I Thought It Was Just Me (But it isn't).* New York: Gotham Books.

Cozolino, L. (2016) *Why Therapy Works.* New York: Norton Publishers.

Crabtree, J. and Crabtree, J. (2011) *Living With a Creative Mind.* Australia: Zebra Publishing.

Crenshaw, D. and Stewart, A. (2016) *Play Therapy: A Comprehensive Guide to Theory and Practice.* New York: The Guilford Press.

de Thierry, B. (2016) *A Simple Guide to Child Trauma.* London: Jessica Kingsley Publishers.

de Thierry, B. (2015) *Teaching the Child on the Trauma Continuum.* Guildford: Grosvenor Publishing.

Hartley-Brewer. E. (2001) *Raising Confident Boys.* Cambridge, MA: Da Capa Press.

Hsu, D.T., Sanford, B.J., Meyers, K.K., Love, T.M., *et al.* (2013) 'Response of the m-opioid system to social rejection and acceptance.' *Molecular Psychiatry 18*, 1211–1217.

Kiselica, M., Englar-Carlson. M. and Horne, A. (2008) *Counselling Troubled Boys: A Guidebook for Professionals.* Oxford: Routledge.

Leary, M.R. and Springer, C.A. (2001) 'Hurt Feelings: The Neglected Emotion.' In R. Kowalski (ed.), *Aversive Behaviors and Interpersonal Transgression.* Washington, DC: American Psychological Association.

Macdonald, G. and Leary, M R. (2005) 'Why does social exclusion hurt? The relationship between social and physical pain.' *Psychological Bulletin 131*, 2, 202–223.

Merriam-Webster (2017) 'Masculine.' Available at www.merriam-webster.com/dictionary/masculine, accessed on 30 July 2017.

Oaklander, V. (2007) *Hidden Treasure: A Map To the Child's Inner Self.* London: Karnac Books.

Office for National Statistics (2015) 'Suicides in the UK: 2015 Registrations.' London: Office for National Statistics.

Perry, B.D. (2002) 'Childhood experience and the expression of gentle potential. What childhood tells us about nature and nurture.' *Brain and Mind 3*, 1, 79–100.

Perry, B. D. (2006) 'Applying principles of neurodevelopment to clinical work with maltreated and traumatized children: The neurosequential model of therapeutics.' In N.B. Webb (ed.) *Working with Traumatized Youth in Child Welfare.* New York: The Guilford Press.

Rizzolatti, G. and Sinigaglia, C. (2008) *Mirrors in the Brain: How Our Minds Share Actions and Emotions.* Oxford: Oxford University Press.

Siegel, D. (2007) *The Mindful Brain*. New York: Norton.

Siegel, D. and Payne Bryson, T. (2012) *The Whole-Brain Child: Twelve Proven Strategies to Nurture Your Child's Developing Mind.* New York: Delacorte Press.

Urban Dictionary (2005) 'Masculinity.' Available at www.urbandictionary.com/define.php?term=masculine, accessed on 30 July 2017.

Recommended reading

Cozolino, L. (2006) *Neuroscience of Human Relationships: Attachment and the Social Brain.* New York: Norton Publishers.

Perry, B. and Szalavitz, M. (2011) *Born for Love: Why Empathy Is Essential – and Endangered.* New York: Harper Collins.

Schore, A. (2017) 'Be Worried about Boys – especially baby boys.' Available at www.psychologytoday.com/blog/moral-landscapes/201701/be-worried-about-boys-especially-baby-boys, accessed on 30 July 2017.

Seigel, D. and Payne Bryson. T. (2012) *Whole-Brain Child: Twelve Proven Strategies to Nurture Your Child's Developing Mind.* New York: Delacorte Press.

de Thierry, B. (2015) *Teaching the Child on the Trauma Continuum.* Guildford: Grosvenor Publishing.

INDEX

Betsy de Thierry is a mum of four brilliant boys, a practising psychotherapist and a qualified primary school teacher who has founded several charities that work directly with troubled families. She is a trauma specialist who is highly sought after to train and consult for teachers, therapists, psychologists, paediatricians, social workers, parenting support workers and the police. Betsy has authored several books including *Teaching the Child on the Trauma Continuum* and *The Simple Guide to Child Trauma*.

Betsy is the Founding Director of the Trauma Recovery Centre (www.trc-uk.org), which is a charity for traumatised children who find mainstream school too overwhelming, with therapy centres, alternative education centres and training centres across the UK. She is also the CEO of BdT Ltd (www.betsytraininguk.co.uk) Trauma Training and Consultancy, which supports professionals who work with traumatised children in the UK.